PEOPLE WHO HELP US

PARAMEDIC

Rebecca Hunter

**Photography by
Chris Fairclough**

Tulip Books

www.tulipbooks.co.uk

This edition published by:
Tulip Books
Dept 302
43 Owston Road
Carcroft
Doncaster
DN6 8DA.

The author would like to thank Candice Roe, Malcolm Saunders, the staff at Craven Arms Ambulance Station, Daphne Lewis and Shropshire and West Midland Ambulance Service NHS Trust for their participation in this book.

Acknowledgements
Commissioned photography by Chris Fairclough.

British Library Cataloguing in Publication Data (CIP) is available for this title.

ISBN: 978-1-78388-038-6

Printed in Spain by Edelvives

Words appearing in bold like this, are explained in the glossary.

Contents

I am a paramedic

My name is Candice.

I am a **paramedic**.

I work for
the Shropshire
Ambulance Service
in Craven Arms.

Today I am on a day **shift**. I arrive at the ambulance **base station** at seven o'clock in the morning.

Malcolm is an ambulance **technician**. I will be working with him today.

Signing in

Inside the **crew room** I say hello to Dave. He is just finishing the night **shift**. It is nearly time for him to go home.

I write my name on the signing-in sheet. This shows what time I started work.

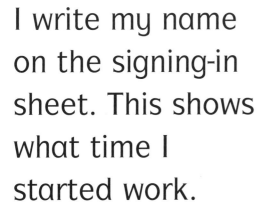

Then I go to the kitchen to make some tea.

Checking the equipment

Before we can go out in the ambulance we have to check that everything is working.

First I check that the blue flashing lights work.

Then Malcolm looks at the oil level.

8

Inside the ambulance I check that the medical bag has a complete set of supplies.

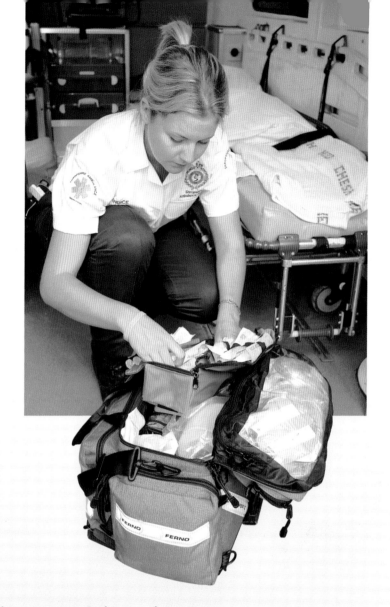

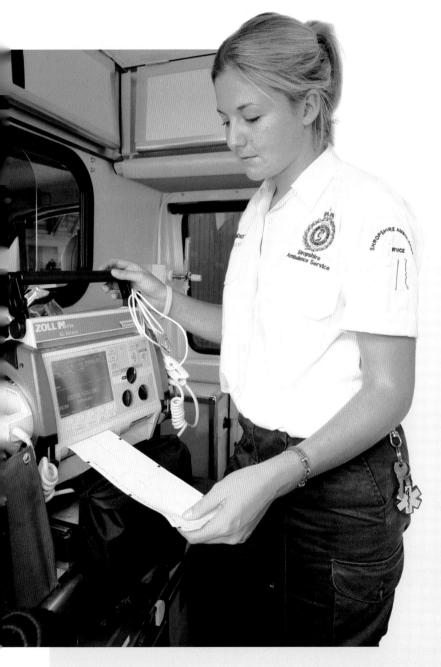

This machine is a defibrillator. It is used to restart someone's heart after a **heart attack**. I print out a sheet of paper to check it is working.

Emergency call

The phone rings. It is Control, the place where the 999 **emergency** calls are first received. I write down the address of where we have to go.

I run to the ambulance. Malcolm is waiting for me.

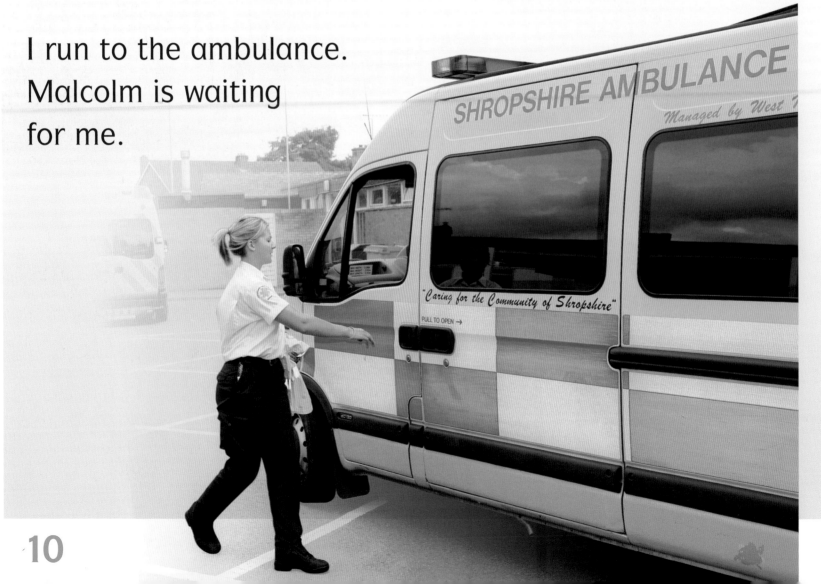

We leave the ambulance station
with our blue lights flashing
and the **siren**
sounding.

We are on our
way to help
somebody in
trouble.

A broken leg

We arrive at a
building site.
A new house is
being built there.
A builder has just
fallen off the roof.

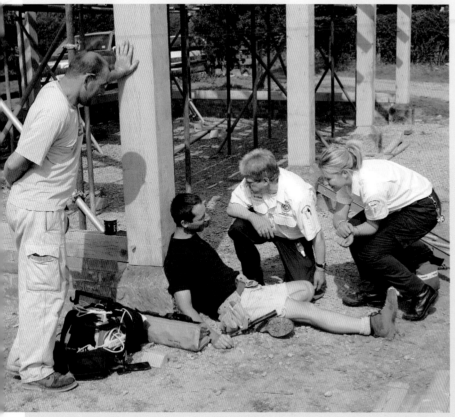

He says his leg really
hurts. I think he has
broken it.

We strap his leg into a **splint** to keep it still. We also give him some **oxygen** through a mask.

We put him on a stretcher and move him into the ambulance.

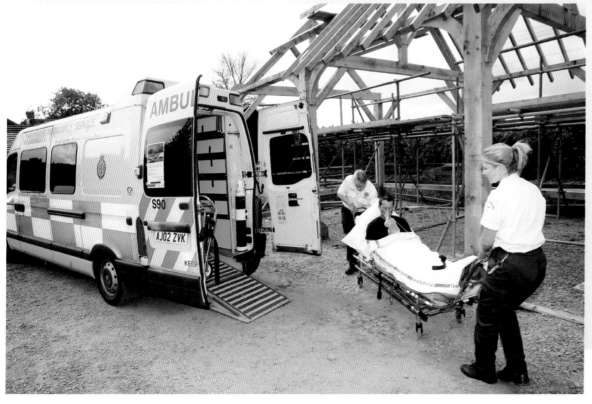

We will take him to hospital where they will put his leg in a plaster cast.

13

Asthma attack

Our next patient is a little boy called Joe. He is having an **asthma** attack. This means he can't breathe properly.

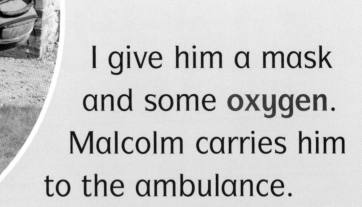

I give him a mask and some **oxygen**. Malcolm carries him to the ambulance.

In the ambulance I check Joe's mask. I give him some ventolin, which will help open up his airways.

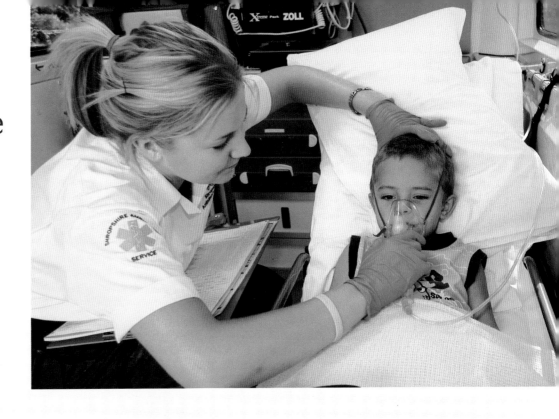

On the way to the hospital I have to fill in a patient report form. I ask Joe's mother some questions about his health.

Standby

Control rings and tells us to go into town on standby. We will wait here until we get another **emergency** call.

It is lunchtime now, so Malcolm and I get a sandwich.

People often come and talk to us when we are on standby.

Somebody tells us that an elderly man has fainted and fallen over.

He is not injured, but he cannot get up by himself.

We help him to his feet and he says he feels well enough to go home.

Road traffic accident

I get a call on the radio. There has been a road traffic accident nearby.

At road accidents we have to wear **protective** clothing. I put on my yellow jacket, helmet and blue gloves.

The young driver is **unconscious**. We put a collar around his neck so we won't hurt him when we remove him from the car.

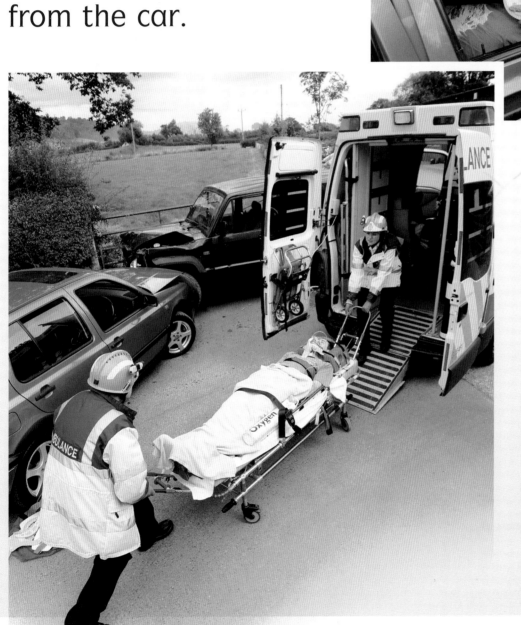

Then we put him on a **spinal board** and strap him up securely. We will take him to A and E, the accident and emergency department at the hospital.

New baby

Our last call today is to a pregnant woman. Lindsay is about to have a baby. She needs to get to hospital quickly. We strap her into a carry chair and take her to the ambulance.

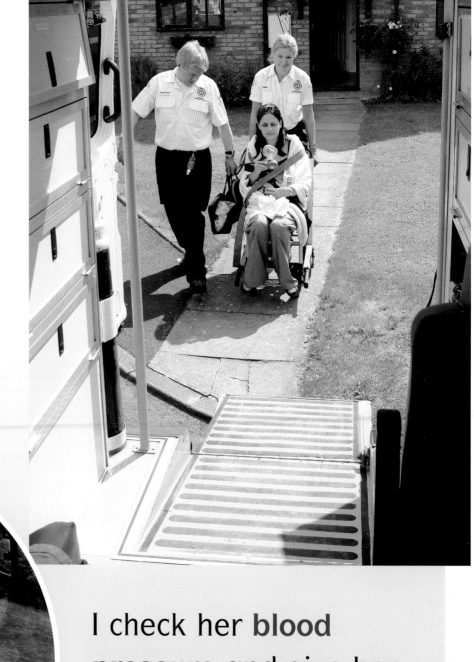

I check her **blood pressure** and give her some **gas and air** from a mask. This will help her **labour pains**.

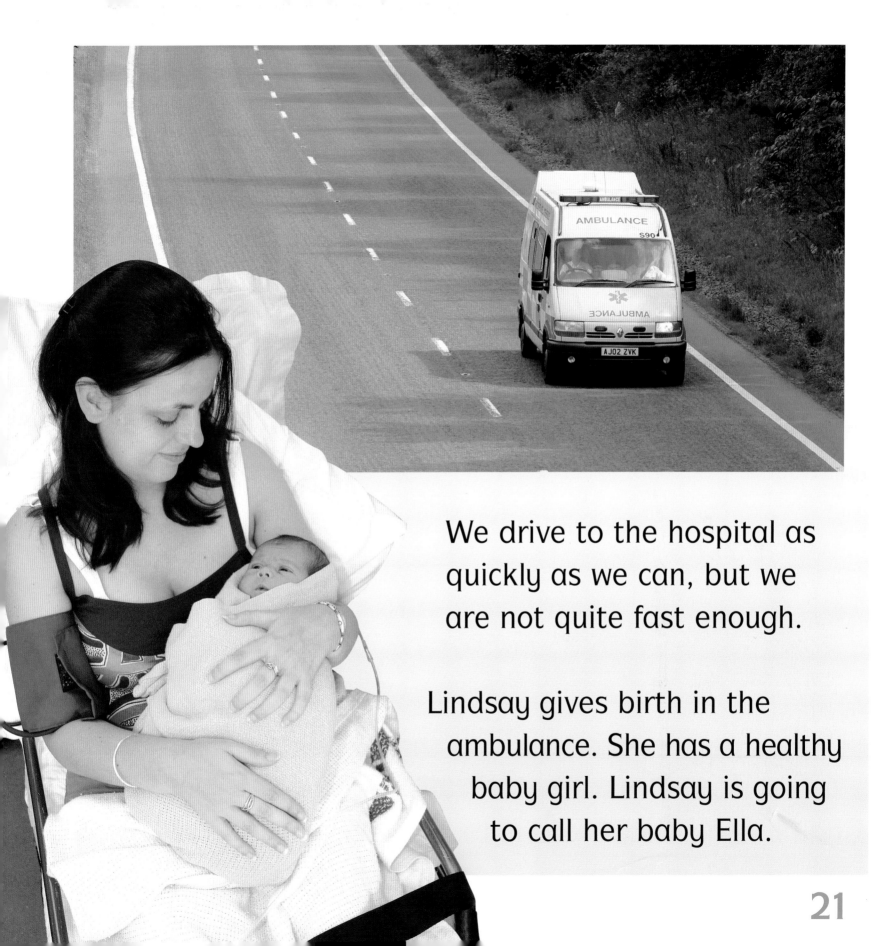

We drive to the hospital as quickly as we can, but we are not quite fast enough.

Lindsay gives birth in the ambulance. She has a healthy baby girl. Lindsay is going to call her baby Ella.

Signing off

When we get back to the **base station** I go to
the store cupboard. I check the supplies.

It is nearly seven o'clock and the end of my **shift**.
The night shift have arrived. After a long and busy
day it is now time for me to go home.

Glossary

asthma a disease of the chest that causes wheezing and makes it hard to breathe

base station the place where the ambulance crew is based

blood pressure a measurement that shows how well your blood is flowing through your body

crew room the living room at the base station where the paramedics can sit, have coffee, read books or watch television

emergency a serious situation that must be dealt with immediately

gas and air special mixture of a medical gas and air to help the pain go away

heart attack a serious medical condition that causes the heart to stop beating

labour pains the pains a woman has when she is having a baby

oxygen the gas that we need to breathe

paramedic a highly qualified emergency care worker

protective preventing something or someone from being hurt

shift a set period during which people work

siren the howling noise that an ambulance, police car or fire engine makes

spinal board a board that an injured person is strapped to after an accident

splint a straight piece of equipment that is tied to a broken arm or leg to stop it moving

technician a qualified emergency care worker

unconscious in a state similar to sleep, as a result of an accident or injury

Index